BASEBALL DAYS

BASEBALL DAYS

Recollections of
America's Favorite Pastime

Garret Mathews

CB

CONTEMPORARY BOOKS

Library of Congress Cataloging-in-Publication Data

Mathews, Garret.
    Baseball days : recollections of America's favorite pastime /
Garret Mathews.
        p.   cm.
    ISBN 0-8092-2561-1
    1. Baseball—United States—Anecdotes.   2. Mathews, Garret.
  I. Title.
  GV863.A1M38   1999
  796.357'0973—dc21
                                       99-10738
                                         CIP

Photo on p. xxii by Jean F. Schulz. Photo on p. 2 copyright © AP Photo/Mary Ann
Chastain. Photo on p. 8 copyright © Jock McDonald 1991. Photo on p. 9 copyright
© Rogo Productions, Inc. Photo on p. 11 copyright © AP photo/Ed Reinke. Photo on
p. 14 by Gerardo Fernandez. Photos on pp. 21, 26, 27, 39, 41, 44, 48, 49, 64, 72,
78, 88, 89, 95, 96, and 97 copyright © AP/Wide World Photos. Photos on pp. xiv,
xviii, 22–23, 83, and 91 copyright © Archive Photos/Lambert. Photo on p. 33 by
Paul Chapnick. Photos on pp. 40, 92–93 (background), and 99 copyright © Archive
Photos/Lebwin. Photos on pp. x and 50–51 copyright © Archive Photos. Photo on
p. 52 copyright © R. E. Williams, The Loft Literary Center. Photo on p. 53 copyright
© AP Photo/Callie Lipkin. Photo on p. 61 copyright © AP Photo/Dave Caulkin.
PRCA photo on p. 62 by Dan Hubbell. Photo on p. 80 copyright © 1990 TV Sports
Mailbag, Elmsford, NY 10523. Photo on p. 81 copyright © AP Photo/Dennis Cook.
Photo on p. 82 copyright © Frode Neilsen.

Cover and interior design by Nick Panos
Cover photograph by Archive Photos/Lambert
Interior illustrations copyright © Wood River Gallery

Published by Contemporary Books
A division of NTC/Contemporary Publishing Group, Inc.
4255 West Touhy Avenue, Lincolnwood (Chicago), Illinois 60712-1975 U.S.A.
Copyright © 2000 by Garret Mathews
Printed in the United States of America
International Standard Book Number: 0-8092-2561-1
00 01 02 03 04 05 VL 20 19 18 17 16 15 14 13 12 11 10 9 8 7 6 5 4 3 2 1

CONTENTS

It's funny what you remember about being ten years old:

The rare elementary-school teachers who let us play King of the Mountain during recess.

Neighbors who had cool jobs, like the auto dealer up the street who gave me model cars.

Saturday mornings, and my father driving from one end of our small town (Abingdon, Virginia, population 5,000) to the other hand-delivering payments on his bills because he didn't trust the post office. I'd volunteer to bring in the check at the natural-gas company because the man behind the counter was always good for a sucker, if not a candy bar.

INTRODUCTION

The big black building across the street from the courthouse where prominent grown-ups gathered on the sly to drink beer. It wasn't wise to be spotted by a member of the church crowd, so they parked outside the barbershop and sneaked in when nobody was looking.

But mostly it's baseball that sticks in my mind: The lot on Circle Drive where we played pick up. And the Little League field across from the cemetery where we played for real, or as real as it gets when a guy named Elwood is one of the coaches and the Mattie Roundtree Garden Club sponsors the best team.

Adults organized the Little League games. We didn't like the intrusion but had little choice. They had the catcher's gear, Army-surplus bags full of bats, and a seemingly endless supply of hardware-store baseballs, and they always saw to it that somebody's older brother was in the PA booth to announce the next player coming to the plate.

It was great. Even if we went 0-for-3 and caught a skin disease from the uniforms that were recycled for up to six seasons, the sound of our names would reverberate across the street to Ratliff Transfer Company, occasionally, we were told, stopping work.

The day games at Circle Field—or Circle Stadium, as we liked to call it—were for kids, invitation only: A.C., Bobby, Joe, David, Dan, and Jerry for sure. And the White's Mill Road bunch, if they promised not to cuss. A.C.'s parents hated cussing. And Becky, if she wouldn't blab it all over school that she was as good as the boys. A kid would telephone a kid and that kid would telephone another kid, and so on until we had a cast of at least six. If somebody's cousin from out of town showed up, he received a quick summary of the Circle Stadium ground rules:

- Ball hit over Circle Drive on the fly—a home run
- Ball bouncing on Circle Drive—a triple
- Ball hitting car on Circle Drive—trouble
- Ball pulled past third base into Dr. Ellis's horse lot—a double
- Ball fouled into Miss Wilson's prized flowers—retrieved as fast as possible because the woman hated baseball and little boys in general and once threatened to call the FBI on the next player to disturb her plant life
- Ball coming to rest on discolored grass atop oozing septic system along right-field foul line—leave the stinking thing alone until the end of the game and maybe a kindhearted adult will fish it out for us

We borrowed our fathers' lawn mowers to groom the field. We borrowed our mothers' flour sacks to mark the baselines. We hammered part of an old tire into the ground for the pitching rubber.

Honeybees swarmed in the area of the pitcher's mound, a significant reason why no hurler had a high leg kick.

Backyard rules applied: Invisible base runners unless there were more than four on a side. No bunts. No steals. No leaning against the birdbath in the on-deck circle.

We shared bats and gloves. We traded baseball cards. We mastered the fine art of wrapping an unraveling ball with duct tape.

The games went on for hours. Batting averages ebbed and flowed under the summer sun.

I learned A.C. couldn't hit a curve. I learned horse leavings could absolutely ruin a baseball. I learned never to volunteer my shirt for first base. I learned how to catch a fly ball after it had been deflected by an oak tree. And, during a rain delay, I learned from David how mommies and daddies make babies.

While I was a long way from being the best player, I did stand out in one important category: finding lost balls. The summer I learned how to throw a curveball was the same summer I rescued Bobby's baseball three times from impossible lies inside the horse lot. I became the go-to guy whenever the ball went anywhere near Miss Wilson's shrubs because of the necessity of a quick find. Once, I was successful at locating a foul ball that lodged in a branch a full six feet off the ground. They called me "Radar" for weeks. But my crowning achievement came the day a group of older boys invited me to their field—not to play, but to locate lost balls. I'll never forget it. I went 3-for-4, including a miraculous find of a ball in a culvert.

The Little League games started around six o'clock, but we tried to show up by at least five. Charley Herndon put two baseballs under his shirt and walked around as if he were a girl, a performance that wasn't to be missed. Buddy Mitchell, who later played in college, showed off by heaving the ball from the right-field fence over the backstop. Ernie Travis, a baseball legend at ten but a dope pusher at twenty, hit ball after ball into the Ratliff Transfer parking lot during batting practice.

Once Miss Wilson came to a game, but by mistake she thought it was where the Mattie Roundtree Club was meeting.

My best friend, Steve Heslep, was the catcher for the Rotary. One day his coach became convinced the umpire was calling a lousy game and ordered Steve to make no attempt to catch balls that bounced in front of the plate. The idea was for the umpire to take one where it hurts.

He did, in the fourth inning. After rolling around on the ground for several minutes, the ashen ump called for play to resume. It was amazing. The Rotary had all the best players and was on its way to a championship. The Jaycees hadn't won a game all year and its pitcher couldn't throw a strike if the plate was the size of a flight deck. The kid all of a sudden achieved pinpoint control in the umpire's eyes and the Jaycees won going away.

An old black man named Smokey was the grounds crew. He would meticulously prepare the field before games and sprinkle a light coating of lime on each base, a trick he said he learned when he used to mow the grass at big-league fields. We laughed at that, and he would hang his head. I don't know if Smokey was telling the truth or not, but by laughing we stripped a human being of his dignity and that was something much worse than going 0-for-3.

I remember holding the ball on the pitcher's mound in a driving rain for a full ten seconds so making contact became the moral equivalent of hitting a shot put. Ernie Travis popped out to end the game and I was the hero. I looked in the newspaper the next morning to find out I had led the team with a "brace" of doubles. (I had to look the word up; it means "two.")

It was Little League tradition for the coach to celebrate three victories in a row by treating his team to milk shakes. Our grown-up had unappealing transportation—a station wagon with his wife's wheelbarrow in the back. We opted to go with Jack instead.

Moochie, Chip, Joe, Glenn, Billy—never had Valley Street known such whooping and hollering. The evening was ours. We were young, we knew how to compute an earned run average, and we just knew that one of these days we were going to hit one to Ratliff Transfer.

Ah, Jack. He lived to watch kids play baseball. He was older than our fathers but not as old as our grandfathers. He didn't have any children, so he adopted the players on the Little League teams.

Jack played no favorites. We were all stars.

Every afternoon he assumed the same position—half standing, half leaning against the fence beside the home team's dugout. He knew everybody—coaches, umpires, parents, even the batboys.

"Howyadoing," he said to the grown-ups.

"Attaboy," he said to us.

You could strike out four times and be dropped to ninth in the order. You could muff every ground ball and be dispatched to right field. It didn't matter to Jack. "Attaboy," he'd holler. "You can do it." The Little League field can be a lonely place if you stink. Jack's encouraging words raised our spirits and dried our tears.

The coach could threaten to trade us for a whole new team. Our dads could make jokes about fathering a bunch of losers.

We knew we always had Jack. Win or lose. Stink or not stink.

It was like he was another kid. We'd gather around him before games and talk about school, or baseball, or even girls. Jack was a no-pressure kind of guy. He looked into our eyes as if what we were saying was really important. We knew Jack wouldn't tattletale to our parents. Or rat to the coach.

Jack had a computer for a brain. He knew how many games your team won. He knew the last time you got more than one hit in a game. He knew if you had a chance to make the all-star team.

The league never had to arrange for extra seating at our games. Three rows of dusty bleachers were more than enough. Parental attendance was hit-and-miss. Attendance of grown-ups who didn't have children playing was pretty much miss.

The only nonrelative you could count on was Jack. He was there when it was ninety-five degrees and Smokey took off his shirt before lining off the field. He was there when it rained and Smokey complained that someone would have to pay if his flour spreader was ruined.

Surely Jack had some kind of job, but he never talked about it. A job meant dealing with grown-ups, and Jack preferred being with fourth-graders. Adults would think he was crazy for going on and on about the home run Harold McCall hit that would have rolled to Ratliff Transfer if it hadn't hit a milk truck. Jack could tell us the same story and have a captive audience.

There was one more thing about Jack.

He had a pickup truck, a big red one. We were convinced that if he drove it onto the field it would stretch from third base to home plate. His radio antenna was higher than the antennas on our dads' cars. His radio was louder. And he didn't care about scuff marks. Pile in, he'd say after a game. The more the merrier. Just don't holler so loud that we get pulled over.

The late 1950s wasn't a time of great personal freedom for kids. There was communism to worry about. There was the boogeyman. Eat this and die. Play with that and die. Parents were autocrats. There was a rule against almost anything that was fun.

So the rides across town in Jack's pickup were doubly delicious. It was like we were doing something that was wrong, but because we were with Jack it was OK.

I played a game with my ball cap, using it to scoop air like a bulldozer collects dirt. I pretended to dump the air and then reach up to get another load. The wind fluttered my shirt, bent my ears, and curled my hair. It was the best feeling I'd ever had. I wished I could ride in that truck forever.

Even coming home was fun. Because the two-story brick dwelling next door housed a genuine, look-him-up-in-the-box-scores major-league player—an immortal status that has never been seen since in my hometown deep in Virginia's mountains.

Gail Harris bounced around the minors for several years before earning prime time with the New York Giants and Detroit Tigers in the late 1950s. The managers never considered Gail an indispensable first baseman, and made him share the position with players from other parts of the country who perhaps also lived next door to impressionable ten-year-old boys. A beanball cut short his career and Gail Harris was out of baseball not long after his thirtieth birthday.

In short, he was no superstar—just a good country ballplayer who could be counted on to hit .250 and not hurt you in the field.

The reality of Gail's fragile standing at the top never hit home with me. He knew Minnie Minoso and Nellie Fox. He rode on big planes. He played under bright lights. What else was there?

I knew about Gail Harris even before he moved

next door. The English teacher at Abingdon High School was a frequent visitor to our house. Someone brought up his name and Mrs. Witherspoon was reminded of a story.

Gail was less than a solid student when he was in her class. She told Gail he would never amount to anything if he couldn't learn at least the rudiments of the personal pronoun.

"I'm going to make the big leagues. I don't need to know no grammar," he told her. "I'll buy the biggest car I can find, and when I do, I'm going to drive it to your house and blow the horn as loud as I can."

And you know what? she said. He did.

An uplifting story indeed to an elementary schooler who loved baseball and hated personal pronouns.

It was beyond my meager scope to ask why a major-league ballplayer would want to live in an average house in an average neighborhood. Maybe it was because Gail spent most of his dough on the big car and didn't have enough left for an estate. Maybe it was because he was a home boy at heart and didn't want to lord it over his buddies.

No matter. One day the moving truck came and there he was in the front seat. I forgave him for not wearing his Tigers uniform. It wouldn't have been right to soil it on the gearshift. I was much too shy to introduce myself. And for good reason. Gail was a big-league first baseman who could dig line drives out of the dirt. I was hit-or-miss on pop-ups coming right at me.

My strategy to meet him involved watching his back door for hours at a time. When he opened it, I would grab my younger brother and play a hurried game of catch, hoping Gail would see us and ask to join in.

That didn't work. He would finish his business and go back inside before Dan and I had time to warm up our gloves. Precious time passed. At the rate I was going, Gail would drive his big car to spring training without knowing there was a not very bold ten-year-old next door who studied his every move.

My dream was that Gail would knock on the front door and ask if I wanted to go outside and play. I let it slip one night at the dinner table, asking my father if big leaguers ever tossed the ball back and forth with people who weren't big leaguers.

Later that night, Dad went next door. He never said why, other than to point out that it's polite to tell a new neighbor which day the trash truck comes.

A week passed. Then came the knock at the door. There was a big man with a big bat and a big first baseman's mitt. He asked if I had a few minutes to spare.

The season is almost here, Gail said, and I need a good workout. He asked me to throw some balls at his feet so he could practice scooping them up. Then he asked me to pitch so he could practice his bunting.

The big brown bat had his name on it. The balls were fancier than any I had ever seen at the hardware store.

Keep the lot of it, he said after our session. I've got plenty.

Then he told me a story. It was the Tigers' last game of the year, he said, and I was sitting on 19 home runs. Earl Battey, a catcher for the Washington Senators, was a friend of mine. I came up to bat, he said, and told Earl I needed one more long one to reach 20. Earl knew I'd probably never hit that many again, Gail said, so he agreed to give me a chance.

This next pitch will be a fastball, Earl told me, and you see what you can do with it. I drove it over the right-field fence, Gail said. The pitcher never knew.

I was in heaven. He had given me something more precious than balls and bats. He had shared a piece of baseball lore.

We talked a few more times, but the get-togethers were always fleeting. There was always some place he had to be. A ball game. A banquet. A business meeting.

He moved before I got to the sixth grade. The last I heard, he was selling insurance. The child in me occasionally looks back on Gail Harris on pretty summer days when I'm stuck behind the word processor.

There I am, trying on his cap and not being able to work my fingers far enough up his glove to keep it on.

He tosses the ball. I hit it into the tomato patch and sprint around imaginary bases before he can fetch it.

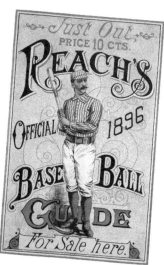

I slide in ahead of the tag. Home run. My team wins in the bottom of the ninth.

Hey, you can't think about personal pronouns all the time.

I asked a number of prominent people to remember when they were growing up and playing baseball. "Go way back," I said.

When you confused the word "bean" with "beam," as in, "Boy, I really beamed that guy today out on the mound."

When you were much too gap-toothed to correctly pronounce words of more than two syllables.

When you and your teammates tried to flush your feet down the toilet.

When you had a favorite rock.

When you stuffed your soft drink money into your socks.

When you asked your coach for a do-over.

When you forgot your glove more often than you remembered it.

When you printed your teammates' first names in the dugout dirt.

When you called your buddies rum-dums.

When you hollered "Candy arm" at the opposing pitcher.

When you sang the "Inky-Dinky" song in school.

When you had your dad run over your new glove with his car to break it in.

When you made fun of the right fielder who came to practice wearing shower thongs.

When you confused the word "recession" with "concession," as in "I'm going to the recession stand and get me a hot dog."

When you might as well play outside because your house didn't have air-conditioning.

When you might as well play outside because the TV only had two channels and there weren't any programs for kids except on Saturday mornings.

When you and your teammates would have loudly thumped your protective cups after victories if only they had been invented.

Tell me a story about baseball at this wonderful level, I asked. It can be about a season, a game, or even an at bat. It can be about when you played organized ball (Little League, for example) or the games you played at the vacant lot with friends from the neighborhood. It can be about a favorite coach or even your favorite place to play. You can be the hero or the goat, I said. It's your story.

Here's what they had to say.

BASEBALL DAYS

Charles Schulz is the creator of the comic strip "Peanuts," which is read by more than 100 million people in 2,600 newspapers. This is an excerpt from his book *Peanuts Jubilee*.

I remember the year we organized our neighborhood baseball team. We never played on a strict schedule, for we didn't know when we could find another team to play.

I lived about a block from a grade school called Maddocks in St. Paul, Minnesota, where there was a rather large crushed-rock playground that had two baseball backstops but no fences. A man named Harry (I never knew his last name) was the playground director that summer. He saw our interest in playing baseball and came up with the idea that we should organize four teams and have a league. This was the most exciting news that had come to any of us in a long time. There were two games each Tuesday and Thursday, and I could hardly wait for them to begin. One game was to start at nine A.M. and the other at ten-thirty. I got there by seven-thirty with all my equipment, waiting for something to happen. Our team came in first place, probably because we practiced more than the other teams, and one day I actually pitched a no-hit, no-run game. It was a great summer, and I wish there was some way I could let that man know how much I appreciated it.

In Little League,

I once pitched a no-hitter.

Our team lost 9–0.

Professional golfer Fuzzy Zoeller won the Masters in 1979 and the U.S. Open in 1984.

You figure it out.

I grew up on the campus of then-small Lincoln University in rural Pennsylvania, fifty miles from Philadelphia, then much more remote than today. During the summers, when students went home, the campus was empty. I can't remember there ever being enough children to field two full teams. But we played anyway. We had five- or six-person teams and simply rotated at bat. I can't say I was any great shakes as a batter, but I was a good fielder. I was quick and could catch almost any batted ball, but I never threw what could be called a rifle shot. My memories aren't of home runs or spectacular catches, but of pleasant summer afternoons on a large field—the campus center mall—with friends you thought you'd always have, playing ball.

Julian Bond is Chairman of the Board of the National Association for the Advancement of Colored People and a longtime civil rights activist.

The Pee-Wee League in Abilene, Kansas, during the 1950s was the center of community activity, the social hub of every boy's world, and the surest way for a farm boy to get into town at least once or twice a week. I wanted that world, even at age eight.

One day, my father told me that tryouts for Pee-Wee were being held at Rural Center School, a new consolidated school about five miles from our farm. It was very important to be part of this new school and to play baseball. While I had thrown a softball around with my dad, I really didn't know much about this hardball business. But Dad dug out an old five-finger glove for me to use, and we headed for the pasture behind the school.

It was a wonderful sight. A ball diamond had been lined out, and kids in white T-shirts were running everywhere. The coaches, who were neighboring farmers, were giving batting practice. I lined up near the batting fence, hanging back until I was noticed.

Marlin Fitzwater (left on opposite page, with brother Gary, and center on page 6) was press secretary to Ronald Reagan and George Bush. He wrote *Call the Briefing*, a memoir of his White House years.

"This your boy, Max?" the coach asked.

My dad nodded.

"Where's he play?"

"He can play anywhere," Dad said.

"Let's try him at second," the coach said.

I ran to second base and stood on it.

"Move to one side and bring it home," he continued, while tossing the ball and whacking it toward me.

It seemed to me that he was forgetting steps one and two—how to throw and how to catch. I was seized by fear, not of being unable to stop the ball, but of not knowing what "Bring it home" meant.

I grabbed the ball with all four fingers wrapped around the seams and clutched it in the manner of a shot put. Then I mimicked the only players I had ever seen—the ones on Wheaties boxes—and took a full windup, kicked my left foot in the air, and flung that baby toward the catcher, which I assumed to be located someplace called "home."

The ball sailed and sailed, and it didn't stop until it hit the side of the school, behind the cars and a couple of cows.

The coach watched in amazement, in awe of my ignorance. He walked to second base.

"Have you ever thrown a hard ball before?"

"No, sir."

He asked how I gripped the ball, and I showed him my four-fingered special.

"Okay, try it with two fingers, or if your hand is too small, three fingers, like this." He showed me how. "Don't put your little finger on it. Now throw to the catcher."

I did as he instructed. It felt funny. I wasn't sure I had enough finger strength to heave it home, although I was at least learning the jargon. I went into my deep windup, kicked my leg in the air, and let it fly straight to the catcher.

The coach looked at me, trying to figure out the kick I was using. I guess it never dawned on him that this was the only way I knew how to throw.

"I think maybe you are a pitcher," he said.

He led me over to a small piece of wood anchored in the pasture that was the pitching rubber.

"Throw a few from here."

Busting with pride, I wound up again. I had thrown the ball exactly three times in my life and had been promoted to pitcher. Splat! Right in the catcher's mitt.

"Looks like we have a pitcher," the coach said.

But it was not to last. I had no real strength and even less control. I pitched our entire first game, which was a no-hitter. But I walked 21 batters and we lost 13–0.

Years later, I asked the coach why he left me in the entire game.

"You had such a great windup."

My first year of any kind of organized baseball was when I was nine. There was no Little League then, but our city park had a baseball program. We walked to the west end of Anderson, Indiana, to play our first game. Dad bought me my first glove for the occasion—a very light tan with soft leather.

After I pitched my half of the inning, I came off the field and the opposing pitcher asked to borrow my new glove. He was a big kid named Chet Porter. I was reluctant to do this, but he insisted and finally I handed it over. He put his big hand in my glove, pounded the pocket, and spit a big splash of tobacco juice in it. It made a dark brown stain as big as a baseball. I had that glove for a long time, and as that light tan got darker and darker with use, the splash in the pocket was always browner. It never went away. I cried at the time, but Chet and I have laughed about it over the years.

Carl Erskine, a former Brooklyn Dodger, won 122 games in a career that began in 1948 and ended in 1959. He pitched two no-hitters and led the National League in winning percentage in 1953 with a 20–6 mark.

CARL ERSKINE
Brooklyn / L.A. Dodgers
'48-'57   '58-'59
2 No Hitters: Cubs '52, Giants '56
'52 Led National League 20-6
2 World Series Wins
W.S. Record K's-14 '53

B ecause my father [Ring Sr., the short-story writer and humorist] had been the best-known baseball writer of his day and was still recognized by many of the veteran play-ers, they would come over to the stands when he showed up at Yankee Stadium or the Polo Grounds or Ebbets Field in the early 1920s with one or two or sometimes three or even all four of his sons. They didn't know that he regarded autograph collecting as a foolish practice, and they would present us boys with autographed baseballs. On at least two occasions I remember, we went home with balls signed by the entire Yankee team, including Babe Ruth and Lou Gehrig.

Ring Lardner Jr. (far left in above 1927 photo, with his brothers) won Academy Awards for the screenplays of the hit movies *Woman of the Year* in 1942 and *M*A*S*H* in 1970.

We had a miniature baseball diamond as well as a ten-nis court in back of our house in Great Neck, Long Island, and when enough of our school friends were on hand to make up two small teams, we would play a game. If we couldn't find a ball or the one we were playing with got lost in the deep woods, we would use one of the autographed ones without the slightest concern about the fact that none of the famous signatures would survive more than an inning or two, either because we shared our father's attitude toward them or because we knew they would be replaced on our next visit to the big leagues.

I loved to play baseball as a kid in Lawrence, Massachusetts. When I was eight or nine, my parents wanted me to take piano lessons. The idea was for a man from the mills to give me lessons. It was the only time we children were allowed in the living room. I wanted to play baseball more than take piano lessons. I can still see myself at the plate waiting to hit the ball and seeing my dad coming down the street. I was saying to my friend who was pitching, "C'mon, quick, let me hit one before Dad comes and grabs me." No pitch came close. I was taken away by the hair of the head and dragged back home. My father said he was paying the man from the mill a dollar an hour for the lessons and there was no way I was going to miss one. My dad made it up to me, though. I remember a night he took me to a game in Fenway Park and I saw Ted Williams hit a home run.

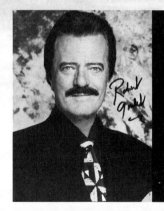

Robert Goulet is a singer and an actor, and he recently appeared in a series of commercials for ESPN. He made his Broadway debut in 1960 with *Camelot*.

Growing up, I was a baseball fanatic. We lived thirty minutes from Yankee Stadium, so naturally I wanted to be a Yankee. The first time I ever put on a baseball uniform was when I played for the Garfield, New Jersey, Little League. The team was sponsored by Mazzo Oil Company. One day I pitched a perfect game. I wore the uniform to bed that night.

Dick Vitale (back row, second from left) is color commentator for college basketball on CBS and ESPN. His latest book is *Holding Court: Reflections on the Game I Love*. He is a former coach of the Detroit Pistons.

Dan O'Brien won the decathlon in the 1996 Summer Olympics.

I was the smallest player on my team in Klamath Falls, Oregon, and usually played right field. I couldn't hit much, but I was fast. Then, when I was ten, my father built a homemade hitting machine and rigged it up in the backyard. He put a post inside a cement block and mounted a rubber ball on a tether. I practiced night and day. Almost immediately I became a better hitter and moved up from ninth to leadoff. That year, our team was 15–0. We were down by one run and I came up in the last inning. All I wanted to do was not strike out, but I got a hit and we ended up winning the game. I was so happy because I was finally able to contribute something to the team. I remember thinking I owed it all to Dad putting the rubber ball machine in the backyard.

John McHale, a retired general manager of the Montreal Expos, spent fifty-four years in baseball as a player, farm director, and owner. He played for the Detroit Tigers from 1943 until 1948.

Growing up in Detroit during the Depression years, all young boys followed the Tigers and dreamed of the day they might get to play at Navin Stadium, later Briggs Stadium. We didn't have Little League or organized teams until we got to be fifteen.

My recollection of playing baseball at ten is that of a group of us trying to re-create Navin Stadium at our local field. Bases were burlap sacks. Stones were swept away and baselines were white dust taken from a local monument factory. Games were played from eight A.M. until dark all summer. A few of us reached professional baseball. A couple of us played major league ball. Fortunately, I have been in the game fifty-six years. My son, John Jr., is president of the Detroit Tigers, so I stay close to the game.

When I was a boy in Illinois, I struck out a kid named Jim Dwyer, probably with my sharp-breaking, tantalizing curve ball.

Mike Downey is a columnist for the *Los Angeles Times*.

Many years later, I was covering Game 1 of the 1983 World Series as a sportswriter when the second batter of the game for the Baltimore Orioles parked a home run into the Memorial Stadium seats, giving them a 1–0 lead over the Philadelphia Phillies.

That batter was Jim Dwyer. I turned to the other guys in the press box and said, "This guy never could hit me."

When I was twelve, I went to junior high school in a busy section of Rego Park in Queens, part of New York City. We rarely played baseball, but we played softball on a concrete field with apartment buildings all around.

George Vecsey (also shown on opposite page) is a sports columnist for the *New York Times* and the author of more than a dozen books, including a biography of country singer Loretta Lynn.

The school held its annual tournament and we were matched against a class a year older. Their pitcher was a giant named Lefty, who played on the basketball team. They were beating us by four runs going into the bottom of the last inning.

Then we rallied, loading the bases with two outs. The three runners are now a doctor, a lawyer, and a dentist, I think. I was the batter. It was all up to me.

I was heavy back then. Let's be honest. I was fat.

All that weight came in handy as I drove the ball between the left fielder and center fielder, and sent it clanging off the metal school-yard fence. The runners scored and I lumbered into third, where I wisely pulled up.

Now we were one base away from tying the score. I had never been in this position before, leading off third with the tying run. I took a step. Then I took another step. And—bingo—the catcher ripped a quick throw to the third baseman and picked me off. My bulky body never moved. The game was over.

I can still remember my sense of shame as I trudged off the field. My friends were great about it. On the six-block walk to the subway station, they all assured me the score would not have been close were it not for my triple. The pickoff stayed with me for the rest of the school year and beyond. What made me mad was that I had not even been thinking about the catcher. All I could see was the short distance home.

I'd like to say that mistake made me a better ballplayer, but maybe it made me a little humble. Now, when a player lets a ball go through his legs or strikes out with men on base, I remember the feel of the third baseman

tagging me between my shoulder blades. Sure, these guys are highly paid professionals, but I try to remember to be kind.

My brother and I, like most Boston kids, were baseball fanatics, and I remember swinging a bat as early as age four. I have thousands of memories, but I guess one of the fondest occurred when I was nine and a fourth-grader. I decided early on that I would be a catcher, and I was one of the few people in my K–8 school who could catch a swinging strike. My brother, who was a pitcher, was three years older. The Baker School seventh-grade team didn't have a catcher, so I ended up doing it. Once he pitched a no-hitter and I was the catcher. We won 27–0. It was to the best of my knowledge the only brother battery in the history of Brookline Elementary School baseball.

Michael Dukakis, (left), a former governor of Massachusetts, ran unsuccessfully for the presidency in 1988.

I played a lot of baseball when I was growing up in Missouri.

The game taught me lessons about teamwork, perseverance,

and hard work. It also provided insights into life off the

field. I remember staying in a run-down hotel in Joplin, Missouri, dur-

ing a Little League playoff because the better places wouldn't accept

the team's black players. I also remember traveling to New Madrid—

that part of Missouri that protrudes

into Arkansas—and being refused ser-

vice at a restaurant there because our

catcher and left fielder were black.

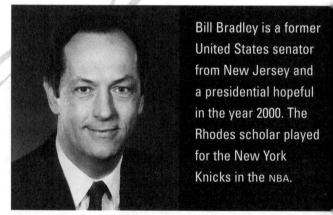

Bill Bradley is a former United States senator from New Jersey and a presidential hopeful in the year 2000. The Rhodes scholar played for the New York Knicks in the NBA.

I spent my boyhood around the various sandlot baseball diamonds in Los Angeles of the 1930s. My dad was a thwarted professional ballplayer. His childhood best friend, Hughie McMullen, was a major-league catcher.

My father became an iceman, married, fathered me, and played on a lot of nonprofessional teams in Los Angeles. Since Uncle Hughie and his wife were childless, I became the target of all their hopes for a kid to raise to be a ballplayer. When Hughie had new bats ordered, he had small bats made for me. I still have those Louisville Slug-

Jack Larson (front row, second from left in group photo above) played Jimmy Olsen in the 1950s *Superman* television show.

gers with my name burned in each one, and mitts of growing sizes.

They made me practice catching and throwing and hitting as much as other kids on the block had to practice the piano or the violin. Like those other kids, I grew to regret it. As I was small for my age and my dad played short-stop, I was thought to be shortstop material. The trouble in paradise was that—though I would never let Dad and Hughie know—I was afraid of the baseball. This was especially so after I sprained my wrist catching one of my dad's faster throws. I tried hard and idolized them both, but their baseball dreams for me were not to be.

ALMOST EVERY AFTERNOON WHEN THE HEAT WAS NOT UNBEARABLE, my father and I would go out to the old baseball field behind the armory to hit flies. I would stand far out in center field, and he would station himself with a fungo at home plate, hitting me one high fly, or Texas leaguer, or line drive after another, sometimes for an hour or more without stopping.

My dog Skip would get out there in the outfield with me and retrieve the inconsequential dribblers or the ones that went too far. I was light and speedy and could make the most fantastic catches, turning completely around and forgetting the ball sometimes to head for the spot where it would descend, or tumbling head-on for a diving catch. The smell of that new-cut grass was the finest of all smells, and I could run forever and not get tired. It was a dreamy, suspended state, those late afternoons, thinking of nothing but outfield as the world drifted lazily by on Jackson Avenue.

Willie Morris, a Mississippi native, was a celebrated journalist, novelist, and editor. He died August 2, 1999. This recollection is taken from his book *Always Stand In Against the Curve*.

I learned to judge what a ball would do by instinct, heading the way it went as if I owned it, and I knew in my heart I could make the big time. Then, after all that exertion, my father would shout, "I'm whupped!" and we would quit for the day.

I grew up in Overland, Missouri, just outside St. Louis. In 1960 I played on an all-star Little League team that got to play three innings at old Busch Stadium. They divided the ballpark so there were separate games going on in right field, center field, and left field. These were Little League teams from all across St. Louis, and the idea was to give every boy at least one at bat on the big field. I'll never forget how soft the grass was and how it seemed to go in every direction. Our game was in right field, and my dream was to hit one on the pavilion roof. I had hit one that far in our regular games, but that day I had to settle for a single. Every player has his memories of throwing a no-hitter, or something like that, but this was really special. More than anything else, it opened my eyes to what the major leagues were really like.

Jerry Reuss, a former pitcher for the Dodgers and several other teams, won 220 games in a career that lasted twenty-two years. He is a TV analyst for the California Angels.

Dan Jansen won the gold medal in the 1994 Winter Olympics in 1,000-meter speed skating.

I remember starting off one season going 9-for-9. At the time, I thought it was because I was a really good hitter, but taking a closer look, six of those nine hits were bunt singles. I guess I used my speed off the ice as well.

For me, baseball was a remarkably romantic period in my childhood memory. I played very little ball, as I was not a sports player. The couple of times that I did I ended up with articles in my local newspaper talking about this fellow who caught fly balls playing a position in middle field. I would say that those couple of games were the only ones of any significance out of perhaps the eight or nine times I played baseball. This is ironic since my father was a semiprofessional baseball player, but what makes my recollections so romantic are the memories of my late father and my brother listening intensely to the radio and, later on, watching television broadcasts of certain games, especially the Yankees.

Kreskin, a mentalist, has made more than five hundred appearances on national television. In 1997 he conducted a séance on *The Howard Stern Show*.

One voice poured from the radio and television— Mel Allen. He was remarkable. He could have spoken from the pulpit. He could have discussed the history of ancient Egypt, or perhaps the evolution of space flight. But no, he was eulogizing and embracing, with remarkable enthusiasm, the play-by-play events of his team. What distinguished him so much from the current plethora of sports speakers was his ability to share wonderful anecdotes of behind-the-scenes experiences as he traveled with the team by train, or sat with them during practice sessions, or talked with them over dinner.

He was able to carry on one or two hours of radio broadcasts when a game was suspended because of rain. I am sure in today's day and age—with all the technology—as soon as the game closed down, we would be suffering through visual playbacks of past games. Aside from the voices of the President and his fireside chats and that of Arthur Godfrey, I doubt if there were many presentations over the radio and early television that had an audience so mesmerized.

We had pickup teams and challenged kids who lived in other parts of San Diego. We played in weed patches, vacant fields, and any other place that was open. There was no adult supervision, and most of the time we were short on gloves, bats, and balls. Even when we were able to start with good stuff, bats soon became full of nails and surrounded by tape, and the balls were taped so much they were in all sizes. But we shared and did the best we could with what we had to work with.

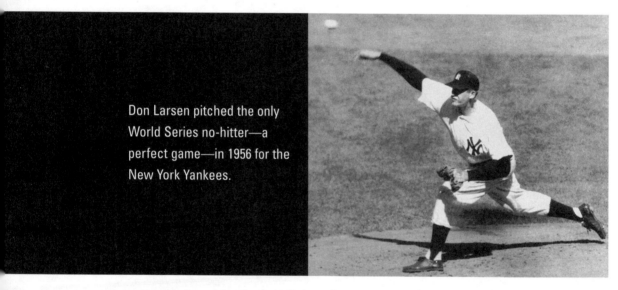

Don Larsen pitched the only World Series no-hitter—a perfect game—in 1956 for the New York Yankees.

My dad was in charge of American Legion boxing, so we had plenty of tape. Once in a while, we had some good bats, but it didn't take long to break or crack them. We couldn't play that often during the summer because some of us had jobs—yard work, cleaning up, et cetera—and most of the time we were short-handed. I can't remember anything special happening. We just did our thing and tried to stay out of trouble.

As kids, our baseball field was mostly the streets of West Philadelphia, although we played some games at the old Cobbs Creek Field, where the games were dangerous because we didn't have any equipment and the catchers were all the time getting hit in the face. On the street, we had a game called pegball that we played with a rubber hose. It was about four or five inches long and you hit it with a broomstick. This was the early 1930s, and usually there wasn't such a thing as a baseball. If you hit the hose on the roof, you cut out another section and kept going. You'd get three swings, and a home run was how far it went. We'd have two or three infielders and a couple of outfielders. At that time, I wasn't a clown. The games were very serious and we'd play two hours a day as soon as we got out of school. You didn't have to call the other kids to play. It was an inner feeling for you to be at the place where we were playing. There were no leagues, no adults, and you got your glove at places like the pawnshop.

Cheese and crackers, let me tell you we had all kinds of games. There was pimple ball and box ball, where you hit it with your fist. We were all just poor kids, and we made do with what we had.

Max Patkin, the "Clown Prince of Baseball," has entertained fans for almost fifty years.

Heywood Hale Broun has been a sportswriter and a Broadway actor. He has written three books, including *Whose Little Boy Are You?* For many years, he was part of CBS's Kentucky Derby coverage.

I took up baseball at the age of eight and gave it up after two minutes, the length of time it took me to take the field at shortstop and get hit in the nose with an errant ground ball. I ended with no hits, no runs, one chance, and one error.

W e had an adaptation of baseball that we played on the streets in upper Manhattan. It was called stickball. The bat was a broomstick, and the ball a rubber ball. The pitcher delivered the ball on one bounce to the batter. As I recall, the batter was permitted a maximum of three swings, even if the third produced an uncaught foul. There was no such thing as a base on balls although with luck there might be an umpire—another kid—calling close plays. The batter, of course, stood at home plate, which usually was a sewer cover. If he hit a fly ball that was caught, he was out, or a grounder on which a fielder got the ball to first base before he got there, he was out.

There were, of course, problems. One was traffic—automobiles, trucks, horse-drawn wagons. The game had to be halted while these went through. Another was the police, who sometimes broke up the game because it interfered with traffic, or endangered pedestrians when one of the players, chasing a ball, ran into them. Yet another was the possibility that the ball would go down a sewer opening and be lost forever. Still another was the possibility that the ball would go off the bat and against a window in one of the apartment buildings lining the block, cracking the window. That did not make us popular. Still, play we did.

Edwin Newman (opposite page, at the plate), a retired NBC news anchor, is the author of numerous best-sellers on English usage, including *Strictly Speaking* and *A Civil Tongue*.

My baseball was limited to the Unidale Playground in St. Paul, Minnesota. It seemed every time we'd divvy up sides for a pickup game—umpire and all—this neighborhood tomboy, Suzie, a terrific athlete, would turn up, hanging around on the fringe.

Pitchers, catchers, and infielders were always selected straightaway, but there was often a problem picking the last outfielder. This is where I came in. I always had to sweat out whether Suzie would be picked before me. And for good reason. After I would get on base with a scratch hit or an error, let's say Suzie would step up to the plate and blast a double or triple far enough to drive me home. It was embarrassing.

LeRoy Neiman is a sports artist.

At the time of my boyhood in Atlanta, Georgia, there was no Little League. Our youth baseball was strictly pickup. We'd get four or five boys together and take a hopped-up bat and a taped-up ball to the vacant lot at the end of the Piedmont Avenue streetcar line.

We'd hit the old ball into the woods, and if we couldn't find it, the game was over. When I was ten or eleven, an ex–semipro player named Blackie Blackstock would pick us up in his Ford and we'd all go to Piedmont Park to play all day long. We took infield and batting practice and then we'd choose up for a game.

Two ex–Georgia Tech football stars, Everett Struper and Pup Phillips, organized a kids' league. I played for the Piedmont Pirates and was an all-star second baseman.

Later, I was second baseman on the Northside Terrors. My predecessor at second base was the future great shortstop Marty Marion. I gave up playing when I became batboy for the Atlanta Crackers.

I grew up in Lynchburg, Tennessee, a town of about four hundred people that is best known for its Jack Daniels distillery. My mother, father, and six of us kids lived in one side of the house that my grandmother owned, and she lived in the other side. I was the oldest. The first five of us were close in age, so I always had someone to play with. The side yard was our favorite playground, even though it was small. This is where we would play our pickup baseball, football, hide-and-seek, or whatever the game of the day was. Our father coached the high school sports and was influential with our sports interest. For that reason, we changed with the season. My grandmother used to caution us about not wearing out the grass on our side of the yard. Of course, that was to no avail.

Our youngest brother was too small to hit the ball, so we would roll it on the ground to him just so we could have another person to play with. We did the same with our only sister. Any-thing for a game! People in Lynchburg have often wondered how we grew up to be adults, because they couldn't count the times they had seen a Majors kid run across the highway and back to retrieve a stray ball.

One of the real thrills was being able to play across the street in Miss Mattie Bobo's vacant lot. She rarely let us play there, so it was a treat. It was fenced in, and we had our own big-time ballpark. Across the street from her lot was a service station. It was a major feat to hit the ball across the street and onto the roof of the garage. I will never forget the first time I did it. I was nine, and I felt like I was Joe DiMaggio.

We had to drive many miles to see a major sports event. Virtually every year, my father would pile us all in the car and take us to see the Nashville Vols, a Double-A team. We always arrived well before the teams came on the field. My father wanted to see it all—how the players warmed up, how they used their gloves, how they ran. I think this helped us appreciate the various games that we loved even more. We never left any game early, either. We stayed until the final out and even watched the players walk off the field. This influenced me very much.

Every time I go to any game, I get there well ahead of time. I want to see it all as well. The most embarrassing recollection that I have in baseball happened when I was ten. We were playing a pickup game in Fayetteville, Tennessee, which was a bigger town. My father was the coach. We didn't have uniforms, but Fayetteville did. It was the bottom of the seventh inning. I was pitching and had a man on third. I asked the third-base coach how many outs there were, and I understood him to say two. The batter hit the ball to me and I threw to first base, getting the runner out. The man on third scored. I thought the inning was over, so I began to run off the field. But there was only one out. I cried because they won the game as a result of my mistake.

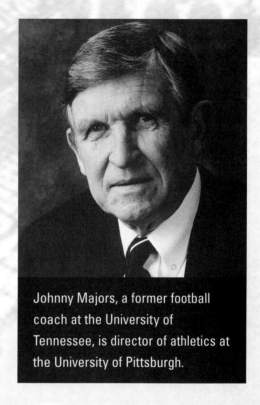

Johnny Majors, a former football coach at the University of Tennessee, is director of athletics at the University of Pittsburgh.

Our family would go on Sunday picnics at any one of a number of picnic parks in the New York area. One of the highlights of the day was a pickup game

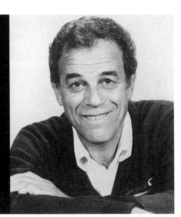

Julius La Rosa is a singer and actor. He's performed on Broadway and at Carnegie Hall. He was nominated for Best Supporting Actor in the daytime drama *Another World*.

with teams chosen on the spot from among assorted families. At one of these outings, I played left field. On the opposing team was my uncle Tony, soon to be drafted into the army. It's 1940 or 1941. I'm ten or eleven. Uncle Tony hits a shot to left field. It was curving foul, but I kept going after it. At the last minute I stuck out my bare hand and caught it. It was a moment replayed dozens of times at future fam-

ily gatherings. Uncle Tony always described it as the luckiest catch he ever saw.

About that same time, I was a member of New York's Police Athletic League, which sponsored groups of youngsters to see ball games at any of the city's three big-league parks. I was on my way, via the subway system, to see the Dodgers and Giants play at the Polo Grounds. I saw a well-dressed young man in a plaid sports jacket and tie who looked very much like the new shortstop for the Dodgers, Pee Wee Reese. He smiled at us and shook his head. But I was sure it was, so we followed him. Sure enough, he was headed for the players' entrance. At the gate, he turned and waved at us with this big warm smile on his face. I shouted at him, "I knew it! I knew it." And with a typical child's enthusiasm, I said, "Hit a homer for me, Pee Wee." And would you believe it? He did—an opposite-field shot to right. Years later, Pee Wee Reese is still my hero.

Mike Eruzione was captain of the United States ice hockey team that won the gold medal in the 1980 Olympics. He is director of athletic development at Boston University and a volunteer coach on the hockey team.

I was eleven years old and on second base. We were losing by one. The kid hit a single to center. I slid into home just ahead of the tag and kicked the ball out of the catcher's mitt. The umpire called me safe. The catcher got mad and started swearing at the umpire, who proceeded to throw him out of the game. While all this was going on, the ball was going behind the backstop. The kid who got the hit kept running around the bases and scored the winning run. One of the adults was angry about the call at home plate. He jumped the outfield fence, came up to the umpire, and they started squaring off. The umpire was my father. The man who jumped the fence was the sponsor of a team. We had a real donnybrook going for a while. I don't know when I've laughed so hard watching a bunch of grown-ups go at it. Order was finally restored and we went home.

grew up in Downey, California. My dad was a machinist, and I don't suppose he ever made more than $16,000 a year. But I remember the endless hours of catch we played and how he was always there for me. He took me to sign up for Little League when I was seven, and I remember how disappointed I was when they told me you had to be eight to play.

Rick Burleson played thirteen years in the big leagues for Boston, California, and Baltimore. His career batting average was .273. He led the American League in fielding percentage in 1979. He is the manager of the Lancaster Jethawks in the California League.

One Little League game that comes to mind was the game I lost 1–0 despite striking out all 18 batters. But what stands out more than anything else were the constant over-the-line games we played in the streets. We had two-man teams, and we used tennis balls so no windows in the street would be broken. If the opposing player caught your ground ball or fly ball, you were out. You got a double, triple, or home run according to the rules we had for how far you hit the ball.

As an eleven-year-old boy, I tried out for the Little League team on the Pine Ridge Indian Reservation. After a few weeks of practice, we were issued our uniforms. When the coach gave me mine, I enthusiastically placed the pants at my waist to see if they fit. My eyes caught a glimpse of the outside of the left pant leg. It was covered with rust from the belt loop all the way down to the bottom. No matter how hard I tried to get the coach to give me another uniform, it appeared I was destined for the rust-covered pants. Unwilling to accept this destiny, I went to my dad for advice.

My mother died when I was seven. By this time, Dad had become my mother and father as well as my friend and mentor. I knew he would console me. I watched with joy as Dad squeezed lemon juice all over the rust stain and began to rinse it with water. Magically, he soon produced the most beautiful baseball uniform I had ever seen.

My talent for baseball never did match my desire to play the game or the professional look of my uniform. It didn't help that my glove never, ever allowed the ball to enter. The fact I was the worst player on the team became apparent not only to me, but to the coaching staff and other players. Just the same, we had a wonderful experience and we all enjoyed the companionship.

I remember one thing Dad told me: "You will find your desire in sports, drama, music, dance, the arts, or academics. I am glad you are playing baseball, son."

Just before the next season, my father died from a stroke. A few days after the funeral, my cousin Butch and I were sitting on the porch steps at my home listening to the

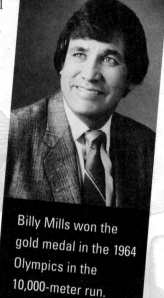

Billy Mills won the gold medal in the 1964 Olympics in the 10,000-meter run.

(42)

sounds of two meadowlarks calling one another. I sensed Butch was trying to ease my pain from the loss of my father. He said, with compassion, "Although you can't play baseball very well, I bet you do something famous in sports."

Shocked, but sensing his sincerity, I asked, "Why do you say that?"

He responded, "All the great athletes I've read about had to overcome hardships. They were either poor or orphaned and people made fun of them. All three of these things have happened to you, Billy."

As those words echoed through my mind, I thought about what my father had told me about finding your desire. This sparked my exit from baseball, and distance running became my passion.

Rick Dempsey played twenty-four years in the big leagues, mostly with the Baltimore Orioles. The ex-catcher is coaching the Norfolk Tides, the New York Mets' Triple-A entry in the International League.

I played Little League in Woodland Hills, California, where the valley girls came from. Nine players from our league signed professional contracts, among them Robin Yount. I played shortstop, pitcher, and first base. I didn't start catching until my junior year in high school.

My story involves a coach I had when I was on the all-star team. He was an insurance salesman when he wasn't coaching. He had a soft spot for players who didn't have enough money to make the road trips, and he was always paying motel bills. He lived less than a mile from our house, and I ran around with his son.

He also was a bank robber—the Jeff of the Mutt-and-Jeff bank-robbing team that hit the Los Angeles area for more than a year when I was growing up. They got called that because my coach was a big man, well over six feet, and the other guy wasn't even five feet. We'd be out of town to play a tournament and they would line up a bank job. Something like thirteen tournaments and twelve robberies. The thing of it was, our shortstop's dad was a police chief and he never caught on. We didn't suspect anything either. To us, he was just our coach and a good guy.

As I look back on it, he did some pretty blatant things. He would play poker with some of the parents, and when he'd run out of money he'd go in a drawer and get a roll of bills that still had the bank sticker on it. Another time, we were driving across the desert near Lancaster, California, and he told us, "Boys, there's a lot of money out here."

The FBI caught him when they saw his picture in the sports section of the newspaper with our team. They went right in his insurance office and picked him up. He said he did it because he always wanted to be a big shot.

He ended up going to prison and died there from tongue cancer.

My neighborhood in Niagara Falls, New York, wasn't a big one for organized youth leagues. We played on and off in some city recreation department leagues, and some of the better kids (that would not include me) moved on to high school and American Legion ball.

When I was a boy, we went at it incessantly on a scruffy playground where the limited number of players usually meant "right field out" rules were in effect. We also played in the feed store parking lot at the end of Eighth Street where we had various combinations of Wiffle ball, stickball, and even rubber-coated hardballs (after business hours when no cars were present) in the gravel lot.

The most important factor in playing in a parking lot is that the ground rules can change in midgame. Cars come and go, and those that tempt fate and park in fair territory are in play. On one particular summer afternoon, the game had gone on for innings uncounted with hardly a change in the vehicular alignment. One car—we're probably looking at about a '58 Chevy here—did select a spot in deep right field, so deep in fact it was hardly worth noticing.

Until my friend Skip Petts launched a deep opposite-field drive that I had an excellent chance of running down from my position in short right center. Off I went, my Johnny Logan autographed mitt in position for a nice running grab.

Now, when you're chasing a fly ball and you suddenly feel a jolt somewhere around your left knee, the immediate reaction is to divert concentration from the ball in flight and turn toward the cause of the jolt.

The cause, in my case, was a fender, one that hadn't been there for most of the day. Now, banging your knee into a

Paul White is editor of *USA Today Baseball Weekly*.

parked car isn't a major problem, not much more than a bruise-inducer. That is, if you don't turn your head, which puts your nose mere inches from the body of that sedan as you move at whatever velocity an active ten-year-old can propel himself.

I don't know where that ball landed. I don't know if the car was harmed. I don't know if my mother ever got the blood out of that T-shirt. And, even though I still don't know all the anatomical particulars, I do know that doctors have a little metal instrument with a flat end that can actually place the bones that form and/or support your nose right back where they originally were situated.

I carry no scar as a face-on-fender reminder. But every time I get a cold and my nasal passages get that uncomfortable feeling, I flash back to that day in the parking lot. In some warped, romantic way, it only bolsters my steadfast stand that youngsters are still better served choosing up sides and all those other rites of the diamond that require no parents, no league presidents, and no national charters.

Just keep your eye on the ball.

When I was nine, I played in an invitational baseball tournament in Frankfort, Kentucky. Before the start of our first game, an older gentleman by the name of Earle Combs met and spoke to our team. He said that he had played with the New York Yankees and was a teammate of the great Babe Ruth. He encouraged us to always do our best. By doing that, he said, there just might be a professional ballplayer in our midst.

Brian Doyle (at left in photo on opposite page) played four years in the big leagues for the New York Yankees and the Oakland Athletics. He retired in 1981.

I was mesmerized with Mr. Combs. I had met a real live Yankee. They quickly became my favorite team. Picture a nine-year-old boy sitting on a cardboard second base in a plowed-under tobacco field, staring out at the trees in the outfield with the wind blowing through the leaves and imagining those trees to be adoring fans waving and screaming for joy at the nine-year-old boy. The boy got up and raced around third base and aggressively slid into home.

Safe! As he jogged in to the make-believe dugout, players by the names of Mantle, Maris, and Berra patted him on his backside and said, "Nice going, kid."

Why use this meeting with Earle Combs and this story of the nine-year-old boy to explain my youth baseball experience? Because it is in the bleachers, on the bench, and on the small fields of our great game where dreams are made. And dreams can come true.

In the 1978 World Series against the Los Angeles Dodgers, a young twenty-three-year-old was at the plate batting for the New York Yankees. This young man hit a line drive that drove Lou Piniella in to score. As this young man stood on second base, he looked out into the outfield and saw fans jumping up and down, waving their arms, and screaming his name. The young man could only think of one thing at that moment—a nine-year-old boy sitting on a cardboard second base in a plowed-under tobacco field. A few moments later, the ball was hit and the young man rounded third and slid into home. Safe! He ran into the Yankee dugout. The players patted him on the backside just as it was in his dream. Only, the names had changed into Jackson, Munson, and Nettles.

Earle Combs was wrong that day about maybe one of the players on that nine-year-old team becoming a professional ballplayer. There were three. Myself, my twin brother Blake, and another teammate by the name of Dennis Rock. However, Mr. Combs placed a dream into some young men's hearts that day. And you know what? Dreams do come true.

No one is too old to dream. Dreams are the energies of life. I believe that if you are not dreaming, you are not fully living.

My first at bat took place at ten years of age. I had been raised on an isolated farm in rural Alberta, Canada. Although my dad talked a good game, I had never seen a live baseball game, and my sole contact with the sport was listening to the 1946 World Series on the radio. We moved at that time to the city of Edmonton—I have been suffering from cultural shock ever since—and I began fifth grade. During PE class, it was decided to play baseball and I found myself handed a bat and shoved toward the plate. I knew I was supposed to hit the ball, and swatted the first pitch into left field. However, I didn't grasp anything else about the game. I stood at home plate and watched while everyone screamed at me to run. To where? I thought. Eventually, I was pushed in the direction of first, but by that time the ball was thrown in, and I was out. That makes it easy for me to remember my first at bat.

W. P. Kinsella is the author of *Shoeless Joe*, which was instrumental in the adaptation of the movie *Field of Dreams*, starring Kevin Costner.

When I was young, Little League was at the Boys Club in Harrisburg, Pennsylvania. I played there for three years with my older brother, Greg. I always wanted to play on Greg's team because he had the best and most successful coach in Ham "Hambone" Hafer—a legendary athlete in Harrisburg. I never played baseball for Ham, but did play on a traveling youth basketball team that won the state championship.

Dennis Green is head coach of the Minnesota Vikings.

The astonishing thing was how far she could hit the ball. Maxine. Maxine Turnovan.

I had just turned eight—the youngest kid, the smallest kid, and this was street ball. The Buick was first, Joey Turnovan's hat (he was 11) was second, the fire

Actor David Birney was the star of the TV comedy *Bridget Loves Bernie.*

hydrant was third, and home was the big manhole cover. The older boys played their own game on the softball field near the recreation hall. A group of smaller kids got together each afternoon after school late that spring as it began to warm and the light grew longer. We were all from the nearest three streets in the projects, gathered to play ball until it was too dark to see or until we were called for dinner. It was a great time. And it was the spring of the year when the Cleveland Indians won the pennant, so excitement, something like hope, was in the air all around us.

Being the smallest boy in the group, I was thrilled. It was the first time I'd ever been included, ever felt part of anything other than my family. My glove was so new it didn't have a pocket, even though Jack Kelly had showed me how to drench it with oil and then wrap it around a league ball with big rubber bands. I'd kept it that way since I got it at Christmas. It had Lou Boudreau's name written on the heel of the glove. I used to practice copying his name in my notebook. Lou Boudreau.

When it finally got warm enough to play, I started wrapping it each night and unwrapping it the next afternoon, hoping that a pocket had formed overnight. It hadn't. I rewrapped it again before I went to bed. But my hand was small and the glove was big. It stayed a giant, stiff, leather claw on my hand. No pocket. But I didn't care. I had Lou Boudreau's glove.

I couldn't wait to get to that game, skipping my mom's snack after school, clattering out the door and sprinting to the corner of Gifford Avenue and Sixty-third Street. Hoping to be chosen.

Maxine was the oldest kid—thirteen, maybe even fourteen—a kind of unofficial baby-sitter/big sister/umpire of the street. She and her girlfriend watched from the porch step. They were looking after her younger brothers playing in the tiny yard off to the side of the porch until her mother got home from work.

I don't remember exactly how or when, but gradually Maxine joined the game. So did her friend. She played, well, like a girl, but that was OK actually. None of us was really any good either, hardly ready for the game on the real field at the recreation hall. And I really liked it when Judy played, because she hit the ball even worse than I did. I was pleased if I managed to connect. And getting on base was an event. A trophy to take home to dinner.

But Maxine could hit the ball. She was bigger than we were, a lot bigger than I was. And solid. Not pretty really, but sure-looking, calm, kind, but she wouldn't take any mouth, either. You knew she meant what she said and would or could do it. She had a wide face, big, dark eyes, and short, curly, light-brown hair that bounced up and down around her neck when she ran.

She rolled the sleeves of her short-sleeved blouse up twice and her arms were so pretty. It was the way she swung, though, smooth and through with a big stride into the ball, and the way she stood looking after the ball after she hit it, the bat cocked in a big arc behind her left shoulder, her head tilted, the way you watch the curve of a bird's flight. So still. And the ball, flying slowly higher, higher than the project houses out beyond Bucyrus Avenue and well into the broad shadowy grass between the yards, far over any imaginary outfield fence. A homer for sure.

It was simple. It was glory. So powerful and full of ease. Dreamy and silent. And right there for us in the late-spring light. We all knew it was so beautiful. We didn't even jump up and down or cheer. We just watched. God, it just lifted your heart.

I don't know what happened to Maxine. I hope she moved to the country and married a great guy and raised five wonderful kids.

And maybe she taught them to hit like she did. I hope so.

(55)

Our team got into a national tournament held in Hershey, Pennsylvania, and we took one of those old school buses without much padding and rode it all the way from Chicago Heights. Chuck Berry had a hit record called "Maybelline" at that time, and I remember a group of us singing it as we headed down the highway.

As we got closer to the city limits, you could smell the chocolate. And it seemed like everything even looked like chocolate.

We won the tournament. I pitched against a team from Puerto Rico, and they had a catcher named Bateman who looked like he was twenty-five years old. In the last inning, the bases were loaded with two outs when he stepped up to the plate. I struck him out to win the game. That was a thrill.

But the thing I remember most was the people who ran the tournament taking us on a tour of the chocolate plant and we got samples of everything they made.

When you're growing up, that's something that really makes an impression.

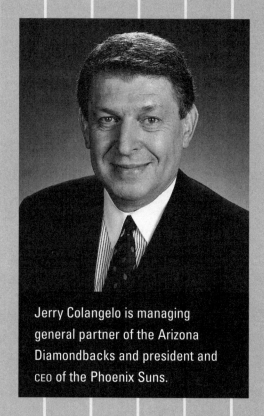

Jerry Colangelo is managing general partner of the Arizona Diamondbacks and president and CEO of the Phoenix Suns.

When I was ten, I wanted to play on my grammar school baseball team so bad I'd go to bed every night and dream about it. Those were the days long before Little League, and there were no tryouts. Team members were selected mostly on a clique basis by class buddies who had played together since the first grade, and they naturally assumed there was no one else in the class who could catch or bat as well as they.

The times when the team was short of players due to chicken pox or measles, I'd beg to substitute, but the team captain—his name was Buzzy Bennett—always picked someone else.

Bestselling author Clive Cussler (opposite page, with his mother at age 11) wrote *Raise the Titanic*. A member of the New York Explorers Club, he has helped discover numerous shipwrecks.

Undaunted, I went home and attacked the problem as if it were a war. I began by coaxing my dad into being my trainer. We lived on a hill, and Dad would stand at the top and hit balls while I waited at the bottom to catch them. This gave the illusion that the balls were coming from a far distance at a staggering height.

I couldn't afford a mitt. This was the Depression, and every cent counted. I learned to catch with my bare hands. I soon built up calluses, but not before I bent fingers, sprained a wrist, and tore off fingernails. But before long, very few lofted balls got past me.

Then I had a stroke of luck. A college student who lived just up the block from me played baseball at a nearby city college. He caught fly balls with me and showed me how to hit. His name was Ralph Kiner, a guy who later had an outstanding major-league career and became a broadcaster.

The day finally came when our class team was scheduled to play the team from the class above us. When you're ten, a kid who is eleven looks as big as a mountain and twice as athletic. The whole school turned out, and everybody expected our guys to lose in a rout. I begged to play, but was totally ignored. There was a little blond girl I wanted to impress, but since I wasn't on the team she didn't give me the time of day.

Then, in the middle of the third with the score nothing to nothing, our team's first baseman was knocked flat by a runner and cracked a rib. Buzzy brought in his right fielder to play first. He then looked around the crowd. Finding no one who looked like he could throw a ball, he stared a long minute at me.

"Okay, Cussler," he finally said. "Go play right field. You should be all right. Nobody ever hits 'em out there."

I ran to the position, still without a glove.

The fourth inning looked like the start of a massacre. We got two outs, but the big guys loaded the bases. The next batter looked like a cross between Babe Ruth and Roger Maris. The impact with the bat sounded like a cannon shot and the ball lifted high in the air. Like a movie in slow motion, every eye on every face was on the ball. I began running back. I stole a glance at the kid in center field. He was just standing there. Now that I recall, he was eating a candy bar.

I ran. Oh, God, how I ran. Out of the corner of one eye I saw the chain-link fence coming closer. I ran two more steps and then jumped. I felt the fence become one with my right hip and shoulder. The ball smacked into my open hand. I had made a one-handed catch of a ball that should have been a home run. And without the help of a mitt.

There was stunned silence on the school ground. Plays like that just didn't happen in grammar school. The months of perseverance with the able assistance of Dad and Ralph Kiner had paid off. The force was now mine. I walked from right field to the bench, slowly tossing the ball up and down, trying to look cool. Only when I passed near home plate did I nonchalantly flip the ball to the opposing pitcher.

Nor did it stop there. I went on that day to hit a single and a triple. Sure, we lost, 6–3, but I was still the hero of the hour.

And the little blond girl who ignored me before the game? Her name was Joy, and she became the first girl I ever kissed.

Professional golfer Tom Watson won the Masters and British Open in 1977 and the U.S. Open in 1982.

Baseball has always been a large part of my life, even though my actual playing experience was limited. After learning to play the game in my neighborhood with my older brother and his friends, I joined a Midget C baseball team and played center field. It was called the Henhouse Chicks. We weren't too successful on the field, but it was sure fun. The following year, I tried out for a Midget B team and was cut, setting the stage for me to try another sport—golf. Even though I missed the opportunity to get better at baseball, I am grateful for being cut so I could pursue golf.

I remember being the only seven-year-old in Little League who truly chewed real tobacco. I also remember all the neighbor kids meeting at my house to play. We even had a home-plate umpire who would wear a construction hat we got from a friend's dad. He wired on some wire mesh for a face mask and then stood behind a piece of ply-wood to call balls and strikes. We were all best of friends and we played every week, but I never remember when it didn't end in a fistfight over the rules or a call that we couldn't agree on. I'm glad we have all learned how to deal with controversy better over the years.

Ty Murray won his first professional rodeo cowboy championship in 1989.

We played baseball at the one-room school I attended near Albion, Indiana. There were eight grades and about twenty-five students. There usually were about a dozen boys, ranging in age from six to fifteen. We never had enough for two teams, even when a girl or two would join the group. So we had a system of rotation. When the batter struck out or was tagged out, he took his place in the field and rotated up through a series of priorities until he came to bat again.

We seldom had a regulation baseball. They cost money, which was a scarce item in those years. Our baseballs were made out of men's socks. We would unravel the sock and wind the thread tightly around a hard core—usually a piece of wood—until it was the size of a baseball. Then we would stitch the outside of the ball with a strong cord that could withstand the swat of the bat.

When I was in the first and second grade, the older boys thought I was too young to play. So I bribed my way onto the team by furnishing the "baseball," which had been made by my parents or my grandfather. The baseball would get wet and never lasted very long. Mother and Grandpop would make three or four balls a season until we exhausted our supply of used socks.

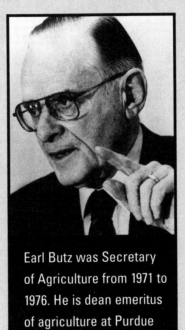

Earl Butz was Secretary of Agriculture from 1971 to 1976. He is dean emeritus of agriculture at Purdue University in Indiana.

When I was nine, I played for the Franklin Paint Bulldogs in Little Rock, Arkansas. That was the first team I played on where there were real uniforms. Blue pants, I'll never forget it. Before that, we just wore jeans and T-shirts. The games were played on the Lamar Porterfield Field across the street from the grammar school, and they went on all day. I'd make spending money by selling cold drinks.

Men from the Boys Club were coaches. One of the umpires was named Bill Valentine. When I got to the big leagues, so did he. I played in several games for the Orioles in which he was the umpire.

We played on our own back then, not like it is now when the parents do all the organizing. The way kids are now, if you don't have full uniforms and shoes, well, forget it. I think you can learn more when you play pickup games like we did. You appreciate what you have. If a bat broke, we'd tack it and then tape it and go on playing.

Brooks Robinson, a former third baseman for the Baltimore Orioles, was named to the Hall of Fame in 1983, his first year of eligibility. He hit 268 home runs in a career that lasted from 1955 until 1977.

Growing up, I organized the Freeport, New York, Barons, who played in the Kiwanis League. Two years in a row, in the late 1940s, we won the New York State Championship, the first year playing the championship game in the Polo Grounds, the second year in Ebbets Field. I played briefly and without distinction at the Polo Grounds. I played most of the game and without distinction at Ebbets Field. But it still thrills me to say I played in those ballparks, even without distinction.

What I remember best about the Barons is one of our players who was the son of immigrant parents who barely spoke English. Each week, I would call his home to let him know when and where our next game was, and each week his mother would say to me, "Who's calling?" and I would say, "Dick Schaap," and she would say, "Big Shot?" and I would say, "No, Dick Schaap," and she would again say, "Big Shot?" Her son, whose English at the time was not much better than his mother's, was terrified when we went into New York to play a championship game. He was afraid that the tunnel under the East River would collapse and we would all be drowned.

Years later, I renewed acquaintances with that kid who could barely speak English. He had become an actor. He did Shakespeare in Louisville, Kentucky, and he had a small part in a Herb Gardner play on Broadway. I was delighted to see that one of us had made it to the big leagues.

Dick Schaap is the host of *The Sports Reporters* on ESPN and of *One-on-One with Dick Schaap* on the Classic Sports Network. He is also the author of thirty-two books.

Eli Wallach is a veteran actor who starred in such films as *The Misfits* and *The Good, the Bad and the Ugly*.

As a kid I used to play stickball on the streets of Little Italy in Brooklyn. The trick was to hit a small ball with the top end of a broomstick. Make it go farther than two sewer covers and you were considered a Babe Ruth.

Later, I was a catcher—no mask, no helmet, no uniform—and I have a nose to prove it.

I was on a team called the Indians and had a Herb Score–model glove, named for a player who went on to get hit in the eye by a baseball.

I particularly remember this one game: I was in deep right field, of course, and there were two out in the bottom of the last inning with the tying run on base, and Gerry Sinnott, who already had to shave, was at bat. As I stood there waiting for the pitch, I dreamed a dream that millions of other kids have dreamt: that someday I would grow up and I wouldn't have to be in Little League anymore. In the interim, my feelings could best be summed up by the statement "Oh, please, please, please, God, don't let Gerry Sinnott hit the ball to me."

And of course God, who as you know has a terrific sense of humor, had

Gerry Sinnott hit the ball to me. Here is what happened in the next few seconds: Outside of my body, hundreds of spectators, thousands of spectators, arrived at the ball field at that very instant via chartered buses from distant cities to see if I could catch the ball. Inside my body, my brain cells hastily

Dave Barry, a columnist on the *Miami Herald,* is a best-selling author. Among his books are *Dave Barry's Guide to Guys* and *Dave Barry Turns 50.* This recollection is taken from a column he wrote about playing ball.

met and came up with a Plan of Action, which they announced to the rest of the body parts. "Listen up, everybody!" they shouted. "We're going to MISS THE BALL! Let's get cracking!"

Instantly my entire body sprang into action, like a complex, sophisticated machine operated by earthworms. The command flashed down from Motor Control to my legs: "GET READY TO RUN!" And soon the excited reply flashed back: "WHICH LEG FIRST?!" Before Motor Control could issue a ruling, an urgent message came in from Vision Central, reporting that the ball had already gone by. In fact, it was now a good thirty to forty yards behind my body, rolling into the infield of the adjacent field. Motor Control, reacting quickly to this surprising new input, handled the pressure coolly and decisively, snapping out the command "OK! We're going to FALL DOWN!" And my body lunged violently sideways, in the direction opposite the side the ball had passed a full two seconds earlier, flopping onto the ground like some pathetic spawning salmon whose central nervous system had been

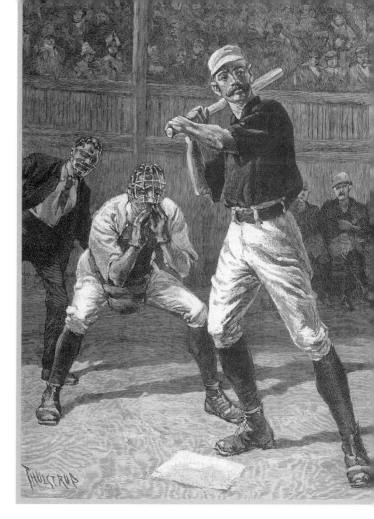

destroyed by toxic waste, as Gerry Sinnott cruised home.

Not being very tall or strong at that time, I developed into a line-drive hitter. This game for the championship drew a large crowd, including my dad, an avid sportsman but one who had never seen one of my games. I came up in the bottom of the seventh inning with the bases loaded. I drilled one to left center all the way to the wall. As I rounded second, the second baseman tripped me. I didn't try for third or home, but I was a hero. After the game, my father said, "If you would have avoided him, you could have had a triple." He was never satisfied.

Monty Hall was host of the long-running game show *Let's Make a Deal*. He also has starred in his own variety-show specials on ABC.

I could catch a thrown ball and about 50 percent of the ground balls, if they were hit directly at me. My range was two feet either way. As a hitter, I could hit a slow pitch down the middle. Anything else was a pitiful swing and a miss.

Former senator Thomas Eagleton (shown here at age 12, with his father at the Cardinals' spring-training camp) was, for a time, George McGovern's vice presidential choice in the 1972 election.

Gil McDougald, a former infielder for the New York Yankees, hit .276 in a career that began in 1951 and ended in 1960.

There was no Little League when I was growing up in San Francisco. As a child, I remember playing in a small alleyway beside our house. It was a game called sockball. We stuffed old socks tightly into a stronger outside sock, and that was our baseball. We would set up ground rules establishing what was a single, double, and so on.

Our favorite game playing sandlot ball in Portland, Oregon, was something we called "double or nothing." If you didn't at least get to second on a hit, you were out. The best games were when we could get four-on-four, but the pitcher was still the one who covered second on balls thrown in from the outfield. The on-deck hitter covered home. Sometimes we'd use softballs so they wouldn't go so far and we could work on building our arm strength.

Even though we were just little, we set up games that made us practice hitting to the opposite field. We'd draw an imaginary line down the middle of the field. I was a lefty, so if I hit the ball to the right of second base that meant I was out. If you had

Tom Trebelhorn managed the Milwaukee Brewers from 1986 until 1991 and the Chicago Cubs in 1994. He is now a minor-league instructor for the Baltimore Orioles.

two lefties in the game, you played on the same team so the defense didn't have to move around all the time. We were lucky. There were two undeveloped lots behind our house, and we could play on either one.

Kids don't organize their own games anymore like we did. All the imagination is gone. We've totally gotten away from children being inventive. Baseball at this level has gotten too organized, too high-tech.

I took the mound, at eighty-five pounds, against the league's leading hitter, Bill Russell. With the bases loaded, I struck him out on three pitches. For a minute or so, I stood on the mound, gazing at the outfield and savoring the moment. It did not last long. The next batter, Charlie May, had figured me out. My control was excellent, and everything I threw was up in the strike zone. May had observed that his friend Russell had gone around swinging before the ball reached the plate. Digging in, Charlie May waited and drove the first pitch deep into the trees above our center fielder, Mike Loh, who waited beneath the branches as the bases emptied. The Lord giveth; the Lord taketh away.

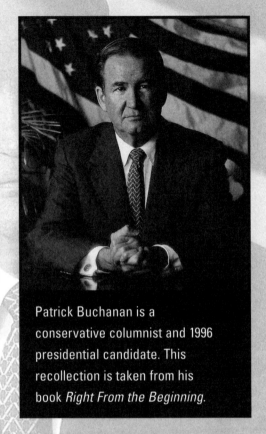

Patrick Buchanan is a conservative columnist and 1996 presidential candidate. This recollection is taken from his book *Right From the Beginning*.

As small boys, we played in the streets of the Williamsburg section of Brooklyn. There wasn't enough money for balls, so we rolled up the cellophane from cigarette wrappers and taped it together. The bases were whatever we could find. Sometimes we could get somebody's grandmother or grandfather to be first and third. They didn't mind standing there, because it meant they could keep an eye on us.

A little later on, teams formed by the Boy Scout outfit you were in. We didn't have enough money for me to join, but my father was a tailor, so he made my uni-

Robert Merrill, formerly of the Metropolitan Opera, was once a semipro pitcher who earned $15 a game.

form. I remember wearing that to a game in Yankee Stadium. There were seven or eight of us watching from the bleachers. Babe Ruth came up to bat, and he was one of our favorite players. The pitcher hit Babe in the head and he went down. That made us all very angry, and we started to climb out of the stands to attack the pitcher. The police had to hold us back. It sounds too much to be true, but the next time up Babe hit a home run in our section and one of our kids got the ball.

I remember a little later on, when my mother discovered I had a voice and insisted that I take piano lessons, I kept all this a secret from the other boys I played ball with because I didn't want to be called a sissy.

We played on vacant lots in the section of Birmingham, Alabama, where I grew up. We chose up sides, supervised ourselves, and never had any problems. We all knew what time our parents expected us home, no matter what the inning or the score was. No one had to call us.

Virgil "Fire" Trucks

All anyone could afford back then was a softball and a bat. In the fields, baselines ran through the weeds and we had more stickers embedded in our knickers than fleas on a dog. If we played in the streets, curb drainage vents were the bases and a manhole cover home plate. This was in Elizabeth, New Jersey, when they started putting in those facilities and paving the streets.

Mickey Spillane is a bestselling writer of mystery books.

Mike Ditka is head coach of the New Orleans Saints. His Chicago Bears team won the Super Bowl in 1986.

My biggest thrill was my first time at bat in Little League. I hit a high inside pitch over the left-field fence for a home run. I got a baseball signed by Pie Traynor, the great third baseman for the Pirates. I cherished that baseball for many years.

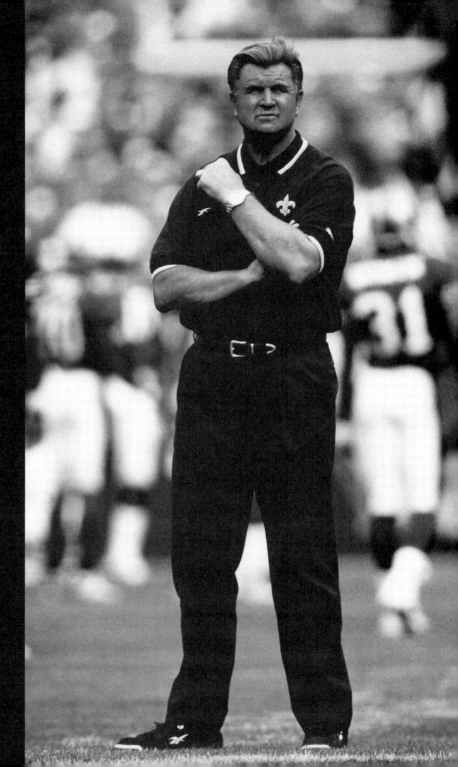

Ernie Broglio, a former pitcher for the St. Louis Cardinals, won 77 games in a career that began in 1959 and ended in 1966.

Playing baseball in my early years in Berkeley, California, wasn't too much fun. There was no organized baseball in those days. By that I mean Little League or other boys' baseball. We played pickup games on the neighborhood streets and once in a while at a city ballpark when it was available. The street games were played with taped-up baseballs. We had to be careful about swinging the bat or stick too hard, because we might break a window in a house. It happened to me, and I had to cut the lawn at this house for a month or two to pay for the replacement window that my dad put in.

This happened in the Khoury League in the Cutler Ridge section of Miami. I think it was 1971.

I wasn't a very good baseball player, but that didn't keep me from wanting a pair of wrist sweatbands that all the cool players wore. My mother said she wouldn't buy them for me until I got a hit in a game. The problem was that I couldn't hit the stupid ball out of the infield. I remember being really focused for this one game, and I swung as hard as I could. The ball went maybe three feet. I took out running as fast as I could. The catcher made the mistake of chasing after me instead of throwing to first. I got to the base before he did and had my hit. The rest is history. I got the sweatbands.

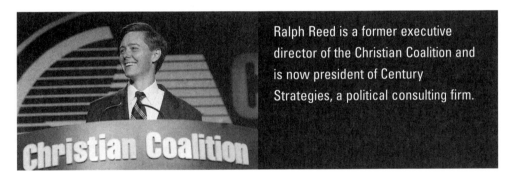

Ralph Reed is a former executive director of the Christian Coalition and is now president of Century Strategies, a political consulting firm.

I remember something else about that season, and it was very sad. We played for a team that was sponsored by a woman who ran a real estate agency. Her son was on the team and was an excellent pitcher. During the season, she was in an automobile accident that left her paralyzed from the neck down. I was only about ten, but I remember distinctly how much that jolted the team. They put her in one of those rotating beds, and people from the neighborhood brought food. I always wonder what happened to her.

When I was ten, we lived about ten minutes from the Polo Grounds in New York City, so, of course, I was a New York Giants fan. Many of the Giants rented rooms for the season in the apartment building next to mine, so I often saw my heroes leaving for and coming home from the ballpark.

I remember playing stickball in the street one day when I saw my all-time favorite player, Mel Ott, getting out of a cab. Just then it was my turn to bat, and I hit the hardest ball I ever hit—a magnificent drive that was a certain home run. I started for first base, looked up, and saw Ott going after my drive. He ran a couple of steps and leaped high to make a miraculous catch. My home run was lost forever. As he passed me on his way into the apartment building, he said, "That was a home run in any park." From then on, I was looked at differently by the rest of my teammates.

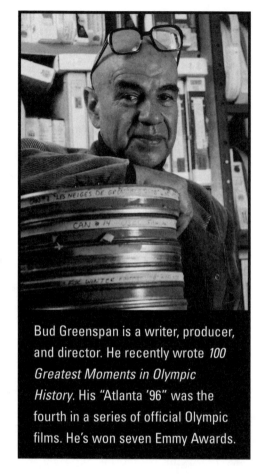

Bud Greenspan is a writer, producer, and director. He recently wrote *100 Greatest Moments in Olympic History*. His "Atlanta '96" was the fourth in a series of official Olympic films. He's won seven Emmy Awards.

I was ten and we had a game against our chief rival. I played center field, back as far as possible. I was very nearsighted, and it was difficult for me to see the ball. It was the bottom of the last inning. If we got them out, we would win. I heard the crack of the bat and saw a fuzzy object coming toward me. I put my glove over my face to protect it. The ball wonked in it. I was the big hero, even though I hadn't really seen what was going on.

Frankie Laine recorded the theme song for the TV show *Rawhide* as well as the title track for the hit movie *Blazing Saddles*.

I grew up in a small town, Denton, North Carolina, and of course there were none of the organized sports kids now enjoy. We made our own games, and one was a weeklong game played at the noon hour at school. It started on Monday, and whichever team was leading after Friday won. In my spare time, I was a busy salesman of magazines and newspapers, and as a prize for selling subscriptions to *Collier's* magazine, I acquired some baseball equipment—a catcher's mitt, a glove, and such— and as batboy for the local baseball team, I got to take the best broken bats home, tape them up, and put them into play.

Furman Bisher is a longtime sports columnist for the *Atlanta Journal.*

I was a left-handed batter, and the best pitcher on the other team was a left-hander, and he was fast and dangerous. After a few at bats against him, I exercised my authority as the owner of most of the equipment and decided to become the umpire. It wasn't that safe a position. The catchers had trouble handling the left-handed pitcher, but as the years went by, I had no reason to be troubled by my reluctance to face the left-hander. He was Max Lanier, and he would win 108 games and play in three World Series with the St. Louis Cardinals. Now, just think how it might have been if I had been able to hit that great left-hander. No telling.

Ray Meyer is the former basketball coach at DePaul University.

I played Junior League baseball as a young boy. The championship game was played at Wrigley Field. Why was this game memorable? Phil Cavarretta pitched and played first base against us. Secondly, I was in the dugout when Mr. Landis, the commissioner of baseball, came in to have his picture taken with us. I got up and gave him my seat and I never got in the picture. I remember that I was bare-legged because I couldn't find my stockings. Mr. Landis asked me, "How come you aren't wearing socks?" I answered, "Notre Dame style." I had seen Notre Dame play football, and some of their players were not wearing socks. Little did I think then that I would wind up at Notre Dame.

I grew up in a shack in Harvey, Illinois, a suburb of Chicago. There wasn't much money in the family, and we had to sleep five to a bed. As a boy, I delivered newspapers and shined shoes in taverns. All this hustling wasn't for me; it was to buy food for the family.

When Little League baseball first came to Harvey, everybody was very excited about signing up. The day came for try-outs and the coaches put numbers on the backs of our shirts. I was a pretty good little ballplayer and got high grades in hitting, running, throwing, and fielding.

Then we found out we would be expected to pay thirty dollars or something like that for uniforms. I knew right then that playing would be out of the question because of the financial situation we were in.

The night that I knew I wasn't going to play was spent shining shoes in one of the thirty-six taverns in Harvey. I'll never forget this big, red-faced drunk who said he'd give me two dollars if I'd sing "Chattanooga Shoeshine Boy" while I was shining his shoes. That was a great deal of money. I charged fifteen cents and sometimes I'd get a dime tip. I was shy, and singing for this horrible man was the last thing I wanted to do. But finally I did, and it was my first experience with people applauding something I did. To this day, when I see someone on television get applause for the first time, I know exactly how he feels. It's the same way when I drive by a Little League field and see poor kids looking through the fence, unable to play.

But a boy of eleven or twelve shouldn't have to shine shoes in bars. It robs you of your childhood. To this day, I think the reason I do the batboy thing is to relive the childhood I never really had.

Tom Dreesen (below, left) has made more than five hundred appearances on national television as a stand-up comedian, including fifty-nine engagements on *The Tonight Show*. He was the opening act for Frank Sinatra for thirteen years. He is an occasional batboy for the Chicago Cubs at Wrigley Field.

The summer I was nine years old, five of us— the Canton brothers, the Kawulok brothers, and I— would ride our bikes to the prairie-dog field, which was our baseball field in Boulder, Colorado, back in the days when there actually were fences, instead of the dreaded multipurpose field that can be turned into anything from a soccer pitch to a tai chi venue.

It was a wonderful field, and we played all summer—home-run derby. Past deepest center field, where no one could hit it, was a netted batting cage, and we decided on the first day of that summer that if anyone did hit it

into the net, the others had to pitch together and buy him a 39-cent Orange-Aid at the nearby Kmart. Thirty-nine cents to us was a lot, and we never dreamed anyone could hit it, so it was a very safe bet.

That summer, all we did was play home-run derby at the prairie dog field. Steve Kawulok kept stats as refined and as complete as those the Elias Sports Bureau puts out now. Batting average, fielding average, home-run percentage, home runs per at bat, it was incredible.

I put out the weekly newsletter, which included drawings of us after hours at the local hot spot as though we were big-leaguers dating Marilyn Monroe at the Brown Derby. But all summer, none of us hit one into the net in deepest center field. I was by far the smallest of the five and had no chance. I was lucky just to dink one over the left-field corner near the foul pole. I think I hit maybe four or five homers all year. Finally, on the last day of a 162-game season (yes, we were committed, we were obsessed, we were sick), one of us did.

It was a great moment. We rode our bikes immediately to the Kmart.

Rick Reilly is a columnist for *Sports Illustrated.*

And I can still taste that Orange-Aid.

I was born in Nuevo Laredo, Mexico. My father was a professional player born in Cuba. I grew up in baseball in Mexico and Cuba. When I was eleven, my biggest thrill was being the batboy for the Cienfuegos team in Cuba's professional winter league. The manager was my godfather, Martin Dihigo.

Ruben Amaro, a former infielder, batted .234 in a major-league career that began in 1958 and ended in 1969. He is the manager of the Rockford, Illinois, Cubbies.

He was one of the few Hall of Famers who couldn't play in the majors because of the color barrier. I used to get teased by all my peers, because almost 90 percent of Cuba's population follows the Havana Lions or the Almendares Scorpions.

I think I was just proud of being a batboy for anyone at that time.

My biggest and most treasured recollection of baseball is that I grew up among the best players in baseball, both in the Mexican League as well as in Cuba. My father, who was a star for the Scorpions, never pushed us to play the game, and had lots of fun watching from the sidelines.

Roger Craig pitched for six major-league teams, including the Brooklyn Dodgers, the Los Angeles Dodgers, and the New York Mets in a twelve-year career that began in 1955. He managed the San Francisco Giants from 1986 until 1992.

They didn't have Little League when I was growing up. We used to go to the ball games at Bulls Stadium in Durham, North Carolina. This is the same park where the movie *Bull Durham* was filmed. We played all our high school and American Legion games there.

When I was ten, we stood outside the ballpark and waited for a foul ball. This was our ticket to a game. Being one of ten kids, I couldn't afford admission. I also was batboy for the old Durham Bulls in the early 1940s.

The saying in Little League of "Batta, batta, batta" is similar to the slogan I used as manager of the Giants. As a kid, we all would holler as the pitcher would wind up, "Come on, baby!" Then, as he delivered the ball to the catcher, it became a quick version of "Come on, baby" to "Hmmm, baby."

As a manager, I used this slang for a great play, or a game-winning hit, or to say hello or good-bye. Even when a good-looking girl walked in the park, that was a "Hmmm, baby."

Senator George McGovern says his late father, Joseph, played in the St. Louis Cardinals organization, "but unfortunately his skills were never passed on to his son."

Author Leon Uris says he was the "greatest unknown left-handed first baseman of all time."

Irving Kristol, editor of *The Public Interest*, remembers not being able to afford a glove.

From tax expert Henry Bloch: "As a kid I loved raw onions, and often I would take a whole Bermuda onion and put salt on it. Then I would go play baseball eating the raw onion."

From Rick Telander, author and sports columnist for the *Chicago Sun-Times*: "In my first year of Little League, my best friend Bill Blair and I had to miss some games so we could go to sex education classes with our dads at the Peoria, Illinois, YMCA. I was dumbfounded by what I learned, amazed and excited, and I never went back to Little League."

From cartoonist Jeff MacNelly: "I was a pathetic athlete."

From diplomat Sargent Shriver: "When I was nine, you could say I was on the inactive list."

From author Elmore Leonard: "There was no organized baseball for ten-year-olds when I was living in Detroit. We did, though, in the fifth grade, collect Blue Valley Butter cartons and sent them in to the company—in answer to an offering they made—in exchange for blue and yellow baseball caps. This was at Blessed Sacrament, a Catholic school. The only team we played was known as the Harmon Street Gang. They didn't have uniforms, but stole all their equipment from Sears."

From Steve Forbes, magazine publisher and unsuccessful 1996 presidential candidate: "The highlight of my grade-school play was making three outs in the top of the ninth as a first baseman."

From Doug Harvey, retired National League umpire: "As a young amateur, I did most of my baseball umpiring in San Diego. It was late in the season, and I had been assigned a Little League playoff game. In those days, we umpired even the playoffs with a one-umpire crew. That means you call balls and strikes and would be in charge of all action on the bases.

"It was the fifth inning, one out, bases loaded in a tie game. As the next batter started toward the batter's box, the coach called him back. I heard him tell the young man to bunt down the third-base line and run to first base. Being an astute student of the game, the batter bunted down the first-base line and ran toward third base.

"I started laughing, but realized I had four base runners moving and pulled it together. The first baseman fielded the ball and promptly threw it past the catcher, trying to get the runner from third base. The batter arrived at third base, where the coach told him to run back to first. The runner turned half-right and ran across the pitcher's mound. The catcher overthrew first base, scoring two more runs. The batter-runner ended up at third base. I heard him tell his third-base coach he should have stayed there.

"I informed both coach and batter-runner that he was out for running the bases in reverse in order to confuse the opposition. I put all three runners back on base and finished the game.

You never know what will happen in baseball."

From Dave Anderson, sports columnist on the *New York Times*: "Growing up in the Bay Ridge section of Brooklyn, we had a sandlot team called the Warriors. In order to buy our gray uniforms with red lettering and red trim, we sold chance books. Recently, I found one of those ten-cent chances (three for twenty-five cents) that promised a grand prize of five dollars to the lucky winner of the drawing. In the early 1940s, that was big money."